PRINCIPLES OF
INTERNATIONAL POLITICS

PEOPLE'S POWER, PREFERENCES, AND PERCEPTIONS

PRINCIPLES OF INTERNATIONAL POLITICS

PEOPLE'S POWER, PREFERENCES, AND PERCEPTIONS

THIRD EDITION

Bruce Bueno de Mesquita

New York University

and

Hoover Institution at Stanford University

CQ PRESS

A Division of Congressional Quarterly Inc.
Washington, D.C.

CQ Press
1255 22nd Street, NW, Suite 400
Washington, DC 20037

Phone: 202-729-1900; toll-free, 1-866-427-7737 (1-866-4CQ-PRESS)

Web: www.cqpress.com

AP/Wide World Photos: 11, 48, 75, 80, 245, 381, 436, 500, 549, 590 (bottom), 648
Cecil Stoughton, White House / John Fitzgerald Kennedy Library: 330
Copyright John S. Pritchett: 607
Copyright Victoria & Albert Museum, London/Art Resource, NY: 64 (right)
Corbis/Bettman: 294, 326
Courtesy of the National Archives: 151, 169, 289 (left and right), 306, 611, 624
Granger Collection, New York: 27
Helmolt, H. F., ed. *History of the World*. New York: Dodd, Mead, and Company, 1902: 26
Kirk Anderson, www.kirktoons.com: 238
Library of Congress: 36, 39, 64 (left), 76, 85, 228, 377, 590 (top)
Reuters: 3, 9, 19, 47, 114, 131, 140, 144, 165, 177, 218, 220, 230, 241, 257, 275, 282, 313, 318, 348, 354, 384, 391, 396 (upper and lower), 417, 423, 448, 452, 470, 477, 482, 489, 497, 510, 521, 530, 556, 561, 578, 656

Cover design: Mike Pottman

⊚ The paper used in this publication exceeds the requirements of the American National Standard for Information Sciences—Permanence of Paper for Printed Library Materials, ANSI Z39.48-1992.

Printed and bound in the United States of America

09   08   07   06   05   1   2   3   4   5

Library of Congress Cataloging-in-Publication Data

Bueno de Mesquita, Bruce, 1946–
    Principles of international politics : people's power, preferences,
and perceptions / Bruce Bueno de Mesquita.— 3rd ed.
        p. cm.
    ISBN 1-933116-11-0 (alk. paper)
    1.   International relations—Philosophy.   I. Title.

    JZ1242.B84   2006
    327.1'01—dc22

2005020664

To the memory of my teachers. They showed me what life lived with dignity is, and they taught me to reflect on how our world works. Though I can no longer turn to them for counsel, still I listen for their whispers on the wind.

BRIEF CONTENTS

WORLD MAP   ii

TABLES, FIGURES, AND MAPS   xiv

PREFACE   xvii

INTRODUCTION: FOUNDATIONS OF INTERNATIONAL POLITICS   1

1. MODERN POLITICAL ECONOMIC HISTORY AND INTERNATIONAL POLITICS   22
2. EVALUATING ARGUMENTS ABOUT INTERNATIONAL POLITICS   53
3. CHRISTOPHER COLUMBUS AND INTERNATIONAL RELATIONS   84
4. INTERNATIONAL POLITICS FROM A STRUCTURAL PERSPECTIVE   117
5. INTERNATIONAL POLITICS FROM GROUP AND DECISION-MAKING PERSPECTIVES   157
6. DOMESTIC POLITICS AND INTERNATIONAL INTERACTIONS: THE CENTRAL UNITS OF ANALYSIS   198
7. WHAT IS POWER?   233
8. LIMITS TO POWER   263
9. PREFERENCES IN INTERNATIONAL POLITICS   302
10. PERCEPTIONS IN INTERNATIONAL AFFAIRS   343
11. PERCEPTIONS, DETERRENCE, AND TERRORISM   373
12. DOMESTIC INSTITUTIONS AND NATIONAL PERFORMANCE   413
13. THE INTERNATIONAL POLITICAL ECONOMY OF TRADE   447
14. INTERNATIONAL ORGANIZATIONS AND INTERNATIONAL LAW   484
15. ALLIANCES   528
16. THE CAUSES OF WAR: STRUCTURAL ACCOUNTS   559
17. STRATEGIC THEORIES OF WAR   596
18. A PREDICTIVE MODEL OF INTERNATIONAL AFFAIRS   627

NOTES   661

GLOSSARY OF KEY TERMS   694

SUBJECT INDEX   711

CITATIONS OF AUTHORS   729

11-1 Manipulating Perceptions for Policy Gains 385
11-2 Strategic Problems in Negotiating an End to Terrorism 403
11-3 Terrorism Negotiations and the Potential for Violence by Hardliners 409
12-1 Domestic Structure and Economic Growth 431
12-2 Domestic Structure and Human Capital 432
12-3 Domestic Structure and Tariff Policy 433
13-1 The Production Possibility Frontiers for Portugal and England 456
13-2 Supply and Demand 459
13-3 Supply and Demand 460
15-1 The Autonomy-Security Trade-off 533
15-2 Reliability of Alliances 537
15-3 Alliance Portfolios 541
15-4 Policy Positions and Capabilities 552
16-1 A Hypothetical Palestinian-Israeli Compromise over Land 562
16-2 European Great Power Alliance Commitments, 1914 567
16-3 European Great Power Alliance Commitments, 1989 568
16-4 Stability of International Systems 577
16-5 War and Uncertainty 582
16-6 The Power Hierarchy in Power Transition Theory 586
16-7 Power Transition and the Risk of War 592
17-1 International Interaction Game 598
17-2 War, IIG Conditions Met, and Uncertainty 604
17-3 War, IIG Conditions Not Met, and Uncertainty 605
17-4 Pacific Doves, Violence, and Power 609
17-5 Types Other than Pacific Doves, Violence, and Power 610
17-6 Arms Race or Growing Organizational Budgets? 617
18-1 The Character of Interactions: A's Perspective 635
18-2 The Simulated Perspective in Germany, Round 3 652
18-3 The Simulated Perspective in Serbia, Round 3 653

MAPS
       World Map ii
1-1 The Holy Roman, Ottoman, and Russian Empires, 1400s–1500s 25
1-2 Europe in 1648 31
1-3 U.S., British, and Japanese Colonialism, circa 1900 40
3-1 The World in 1493: What *Is* Reality? 93
3-2 The Three Routes to "the Indies" 95
4-1 Yugoslavia's Cold War Stability, 1945–1990 123
4-2 Yugoslavia's Disintegration, 1991 to the Present 123
6-1 Europe at the End of the Cold War 208
8-1 How Secure Is the World's Oil Supply? 283
9-1 The Koreas: Arable Land and Access to Food 310
12-1 Top Foreign Aid Donors and Recipients of U.S. Aid, 2004 441
15-1 Conflict between Members of the Organization of American States 547

FIGURES

3-1   The Columbus-Ferdinand Game   109

3-2   Solving the Columbus-Ferdinand Game   111

4-1   Structural Approaches to International Relations   125

5-1   Bureaucratic and Interest Group Approaches to International Relations   158

5-2   Constraining Agents   166

5-3   Strategic Approaches to International Relations   174

5-4   Two Points of Equal Utility   182

5-5   Indifference Curve   183

5-6   Group of Indifference Curves   184

5-7   Marginal Rates of Substitution   185

5-8   Negotiating Styles and Indifference Curves   186

5-9   Trade-offs According to the Interest Group Perspective   188

5-10   Trade-offs According to the Structural Realist Perspective   189

5-11   Trade-offs According to the Strategic Perspective   190

6-1   Policy Preferences in the Soviet Union, late 1980s   209

6-2   Hypothetical Indifference Curves for Soviet Leaders   211

6-3   Soviet Policy Win Sets   213

6-4   Win Sets, International Pressure, and the End of the Cold War   216

6-5   Issue-by-Issue Candidate Preferences, 1992   222

6-6   Candidate Policy Preferences, 1992   223

6-7   Voters' First-place Choices, 1992   224

6-8   Win Sets in a Proportional Representation System   229

7-1   U.S., British, and Russian National Capabilities, 1816–2001   250

7-2   Selected National Capabilities, 1815–1875   251

7-3   Selected National Capabilities, 1870–1920   252

7-4   Selected National Capabilities, 1920–1945   253

7-5   Selected National Capabilities, 1940–2001   254

7-6   Mideast Capabilities and the RPC Index, 1950–1974   255

8-1   Power Relationships in the Libyan Dispute   268

8-2   Intangible Power and the Risk of Conflict   297

8-3   Power, Democraticness, and Conflict   300

9-1   Risk Propensities   324

9-2   Cyclical Preferences   331

9-3   Single-peaked Preferences   335

9-4   Non–single-peaked Preferences   336

9-5   Resources and the Probability of Winning   340

10-1   The Sanctioning Game without Uncertainty   357

10-2   Solving the Sanctioning Game without Uncertainty   358

10-3   The Sanctioning Game with Uncertainty and Perceptions   360

10-4   Solving the Sanctioning Game with Uncertainty and Perceptions   361

10-5   The Sanctioning Game with Uncertainty and Domestic Politics   366

10-6   Impact of Domestic Politics on Presidential Decision Making   368

Tables, Figures, and Maps

TABLES

2-1   Regimes and Cooperation: Necessary Conditions   70
2-2   Regimes and Cooperation: Sufficient Conditions   71
2-3   Regimes and Cooperation: Necessary and Sufficient Conditions   71
4-1   The Prisoners' Dilemma   143
4-2   Structural Theories of International Relations   154
5-1   Leadership Theories of International Relations   178
6-1   Voter Preferences, 1992   225
8-1   U.S.-Japanese Auto Trade: A Simple Game   272
8-2   U.S.-Japanese Auto Trade Game with Costs   274
11-1   Preference Orderings for a Terrorism Game   398
12-1   Free Trade as a Prisoners' Dilemma   427
12-2   Free Trade as a Zero-sum Game   429
13-1   Labor Productivity in Making Wine and Cloth   455
14-1   European Community Preferences Regarding Tolerable Radiation Levels, December 22, 1987   519
15-1   Predicted and Actual Third-party War Choices   544
15-2   War Participation and Alliance Attributes, 1815–1965   545
16-1   The Major Power Balance of Power in 1896   584
16-2   Is a Greater than 50–50 Chance of Victory a Necessary Condition for War?   585
16-3   Empirical Evidence for the Power Transition Theory, 1815–1980   593
17-1   Restrictions on Preferences for Decision Maker i in the IIG   600
18-1   Austria-Hungary's Verbal Summary Table, Round 1 (June 1914)   637
18-2   Relationship between Risk Taking, War Initiation, and Victory or Defeat   640
18-3   Data for the Austro-Serbian Crisis, June 1914   647
18-4   Predicted Dynamics of the Austro-Serbian Crisis, June 1914   649
18-5   Opportunity Summary for Round 3, Germany (June 1914)   650
18-6   Opportunity Summary for Round 3, Belgium (June 1914)   650
18-7   Opportunity Summary for Round 3, Serbia (June 1914)   650
18-8   Stability Summary for Round 3   651
18-9   Serbia's Verbal Summary Table, Round 3 (June 1914)   651

The Purpose of Alliances   531
When Are Alliances Reliable?   535
Predicting the Reliability of Alliances   539
Alliances, Coordination, and Competition   546
Conflict among Allies   551
Summary   557
Key Concepts   558

16. The Causes of War: Structural Accounts   559
War versus Negotiation: Indivisibility, Uncertainty, and Commitment   560
Realist Theories of War   564
How Well Does Neorealism Do in Explaining War and Instability?   565
History and Neorealist Empirical Claims   576
Other Neorealist Hypotheses and the Historical Record   580
The Power Transition: A Structural Alternative to Neorealism   585
Summary   594
Key Concepts   595

17. Strategic Theories of War   596
The International Interaction Game and War   597
Arms Races, Deterrence, and War   615
Other Hypotheses about War   621
Summary   625
Key Concepts   626

18. A Predictive Model of International Affairs   627
Logical Foundation of the Model   629
Perceptual Analysis   633
Estimating the Model   638
Why Does This Model Help?   640
Intuition behind the Model's Dynamics   641
Developing the Data   642
Model Output   646
Prediction and International Relations   653
Using the Model   658
Key Concepts   659

Notes   661

Glossary of Key Terms   694

Subject Index   711

Citations of Authors   729

Perceptions and Deterrence: The Wars in Iraq, 1991 and 2003   386
Beliefs about Terrorism   395
Terrorism, Credible Commitments, and Strategic Dilemmas   401
Land for Peace: A Credible Commitment Problem   410
Summary   411
Key Concepts   412

12. **Domestic Institutions and National Performance**   **413**
Universal Political Institutions   415
Tools to Remain in Power   418
Winning Coalition Size and Trade Policy   425
Evidence: Winning Coalition Size and Economic Performance   431
Winning Coalition Size and National Survival   433
Domestic Political Institutions and the Democratic Peace   436
Domestic Institutions and Foreign Aid   440
Domestic Institutions and Democratization: Nation Building   443
Summary   445
Key Concepts   446

13. **The International Political Economy of Trade**   **447**
Globalization in Historical Perspective   450
An Economics Primer: Comparative Advantage, Supply, and Demand   453
Trade as a Public or Private Good   463
Currency, Exchange Rates, and International Political Economy   464
Political Economy and Trade   469
Factors of Production   472
Mobility of Factors of Production   474
Summary   483
Key Concepts   483

14. **International Organizations and International Law**   **484**
International Law, Organizations, and Regimes: Definitions and Distinctions   485
Can We Evaluate the Effects of International Regimes?   492
Sovereignty: A Successful International Institution   498
The Purpose of International Rules and Institutions   505
Member Inclusiveness: Trade-offs between Regime Efficiency and Effectiveness   511
Organizational Decision-making Rules   514
Compliance and Effectiveness   523
Summary   526
Key Concepts   527

15. **Alliances**   **528**
What Is a Military Alliance?   529

7. **What Is Power?**   233
   Defining Power   234
   Methods of Exercising Power   236
   Measuring Power   248
   The Fungibility of Power   254
   Projecting Power over Larger Distances   259
   Summary   261
   Key Concepts   262

8. **Limits to Power**   263
   Power and Military Victory   264
   Power Can Be Cyclical   266
   Coordination and Power   269
   Distribution Problems, Coordination Problems, and Power   270
   International Organizations: An Alternative to or Reflection of Power?   279
   Power and Motivation   284
   Asymmetric Motivation and Costs   292
   The Exercise of Power   296
   Summary   300
   Key Concepts   301

9. **Preferences in International Politics**   302
   Preferred Values and U.S. Foreign Policy: An Illustration   303
   What Are Preferences?   307
   Rationality and Preferences   308
   Preferences and Constrained Choices   309
   Foreign Aid, Preferences, and Decisions   309
   Constrained Choice in International Relations: Some Examples   317
   Social Choice Problems: Is There a National Interest?   325
   Common Circumstances without the Social Choice Problem   333
   Summary   341
   Key Concepts   342

10. **Perceptions in International Affairs**   343
    Perceptions and Reality   345
    Perceptions and Trade Sanctions: An Illustration   352
    Summary   371
    Key Concepts   372

11. **Perceptions, Deterrence, and Terrorism**   373
    Perceptions and Deterrence   374
    North Korea's Artful Use of Misconduct   383

Summary   82
Key Concepts   83

3. **Christopher Columbus and International Relations   84**
Columbus's Proposal, or Ferdinand and Isabella's Ambition   85
Factors That Shape Foreign Policy Choices   86
Discovering America: An Evaluation of Political Economy and
    National Security   89
Lessons Suggested by Columbus's Experience   94
Tools and Solutions: An Illustration of the Use of Decision Theory in the Study of
    International Relations   98
Game Theory, or Why You Can't Always Get What You Want   106
Summary   115
Key Concepts   116

4. **International Politics from a Structural Perspective   117**
Evaluating Alternative Principles   118
Defining the Puzzles of Cooperation and Conflict   119
Structural Perspectives   124
Summary   153
Key Concepts   156

5. **International Politics from Group and Decision-making Perspectives   157**
The Bureaucratic, or Interest Group, Perspective   158
Strategic Perspective   172
Constructivism   175
Comparing the Core Perspectives   179
The Three Perspectives Illustratively Applied to Columbus   192
Summary   195
Key Concepts   197

6. **Domestic Politics and International Interactions:**
   The Central Units of Analysis   198
The Origins of the State   199
International Relations without the State   202
Domestic Politics as an Alternative to the State   204
How Domestic Politics Changes the National Interest   206
End of the Cold War: Win Sets as a Tool for Understanding Policy   207
Alternative Interpretations of the Domestic Politics Example   229
Summary   231
Key Concepts   232

CONTENTS

World Map   ii

Tables, Figures, and Maps   xiv

Preface   xvii

Introduction: Foundations of International Politics   1
   Governing Principles   2
   Organizational Features of This Book   5
   The Core Concerns of International Relations   7
   Solving International Relations Puzzles   13
   Summary   20
   Suggested Reading   21
   Key Concepts   21

1. Modern Political Economic History and International Politics   22
   The Fourteen Hundreds   24
   The Fifteen Hundreds   28
   The Sixteen Hundreds   30
   The Seventeen Hundreds   33
   The Eighteen Hundreds   36
   The Twentieth Century   40
   Summary   52
   Key Concepts   52

2. Evaluating Arguments about International Politics   53
   Theories as Simplifications of Reality   53
   Judging Theories   57
   The First Principle of Wing-walking   63
   The Case Study Method and Testing Theories   68
   A Standard for Comparing Theories   72
   Why Do We Need Theories?   73
   The Scientific Method as a Guide to Arguments and Evidence   77
   When a Theory Is Wrong   79
   Scientific Theories Must Be Falsifiable   81

BRIEF CONTENTS

To the memory of my teachers. They showed me what life lived with dignity is, and they taught me to reflect on how our world works. Though I can no longer turn to them for counsel, still I listen for their whispers on the wind.

9777818

CQ Press
1255 22nd Street, NW, Suite 400
Washington, DC 20037

Phone: 202-729-1900; toll-free, 1-866-427-7737 (1-866-4CQ-PRESS)

Web: www.cqpress.com

AP/Wide World Photos: 11, 48, 75, 80, 245, 381, 436, 500, 549, 590 (bottom), 648
Cecil Stoughton, White House / John Fitzgerald Kennedy Library: 330
Copyright John S. Pritchett: 607
Copyright Victoria & Albert Museum, London/Art Resource, NY: 64 (right)
Corbis/Bettman: 294, 326
Courtesy of the National Archives: 151, 169, 289 (left and right), 306, 611, 624
Granger Collection, New York: 27
Helmolt, H. F., ed. *History of the World.* New York: Dodd, Mead, and Company, 1902: 26
Kirk Anderson, www.kirktoons.com: 238
Library of Congress: 36, 39, 64 (left), 76, 85, 228, 377, 590 (top)
Reuters: 3, 9, 19, 47, 114, 131, 140, 144, 165, 177, 218, 220, 230, 241, 257, 275, 282, 313, 318, 348, 354, 384, 391, 396 (upper and lower), 417, 423, 448, 452, 470, 477, 482, 489, 497, 510, 521, 530, 556, 561, 578, 656

Cover design: Mike Pottman

⊗ The paper used in this publication exceeds the requirements of the American National Standard for Information Sciences—Permanence of Paper for Printed Library Materials, ANSI Z39.48-1992.

Printed and bound in the United States of America

09   08   07   06   05   1   2   3   4   5

Library of Congress Cataloging-in-Publication Data

Bueno de Mesquita, Bruce, 1946–
  Principles of international politics : people's power, preferences,
and perceptions / Bruce Bueno de Mesquita.— 3rd ed.
    p. cm.
  ISBN 1-933116-11-0 (alk. paper)
  1. International relations—Philosophy.   I. Title.

  JZ1242.B84   2006
  327.1'01—dc22

2005020664

PRINCIPLES OF INTERNATIONAL POLITICS

PEOPLE'S POWER, PREFERENCES, AND PERCEPTIONS

THIRD EDITION

Bruce Bueno de Mesquita

New York University

and

Hoover Institution at Stanford University

CQ PRESS

A Division of Congressional Quarterly Inc.
Washington, D.C.

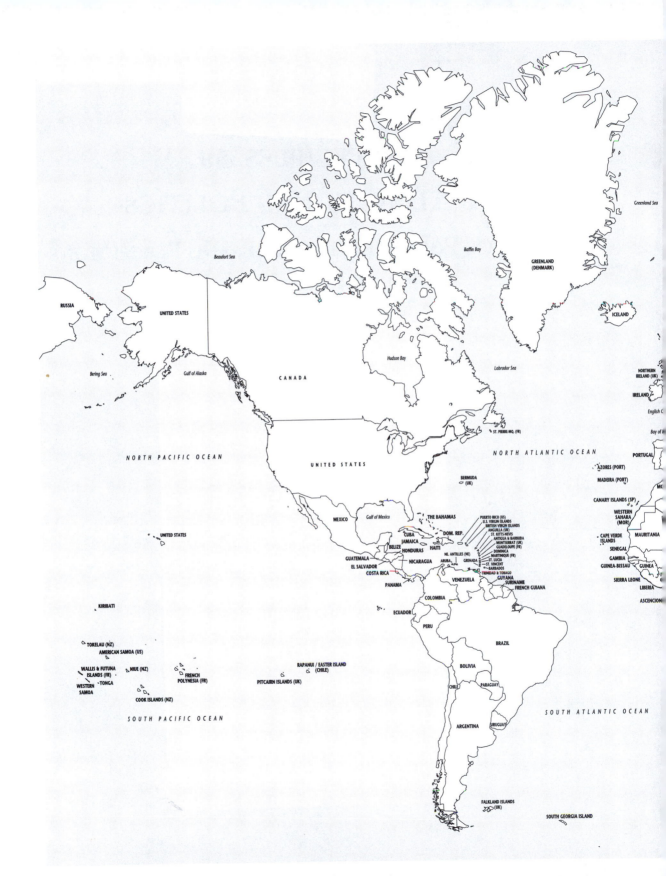

PRINCIPLES OF
INTERNATIONAL POLITICS
PEOPLE'S POWER, PREFERENCES, AND PERCEPTIONS